Come F

BOOK OF MORMON BASKET BOOKS

18 Book of Mormon Stories for Kids!

These child-friendly Book of Mormon stories feature 18 different stories in just 7 pages each, perfect for the little people in your life! They include fun, bright clipart and simple sentences to help your children understand and be engaged in each story.

Stories included:
Nephi gets the Brass Plates
Lehi's Dream
Nephi Breaks His Bow
Nephi Builds a Ship
Enos
King Benjamin
Abinadi
Alma the Younger
Ammon Defends King Lamoni's Flocks
The People of Ammon
Captain Moroni
Helaman's 2,000 Young Warriors
Samuel the Lamanite
Signs of Christ's Death
Jesus Christ Visits the Nephites
The Three Nephites
Mormon
The Brother of Jared

comefollowmefhe.com

Come Follow Me FHE
BOOK OF MORMON BASKET BOOK

Nephi gets the Brass Plates

Lehi told his sons the Lord wanted them to go back to Jerusalem to get the brass plates from Laban. Laman and Lemuel did not want to go, they thought it would be too hard. Nephi wanted to obey the Lord, he knew the Lord would help them.

1

Laman, Lemuel, Sam and Nephi traveled back to Jerusalem to get the plates. Laman tried getting the plates from Laban, but Laban was angry and tried to have Laman killed.

Nephi and his brothers went to their old home to get their gold and silver they had left. They were going to try and exchange their riches for the brass plates. Laban saw their riches and wanted it for himself; he kicked Nephi and his brothers out. Laban told his men to kill Nephi and his brothers.

They ran away and hid in a cave. Laman and Lemuel were angry with Nephi. Laman and Lemuel beat Nephi and Sam with a stick. An angel came and told Laman and Lemuel to stop. He told them the Lord would help them get the plates.

Nephi told his brothers to have more faith. Nephi went into the city that night toward Laban's house. On the way he found Laban drunk on the ground. Nephi picked up Laban's sword. The Holy Ghost told Nephi to kill Laban. Nephi did not want to. The Holy Ghost told Nephi again to kill Laban so he could get the brass plates.

Nephi obeyed the Holy Ghost. He then put on Laban's clothes and armor. He went to Laban's house and asked Zoram for the plates. Nephi looked and sounded like Laban. Zoram gave the plates to Nephi. Nepih told Zoram to come with him.

When Nephi and Zoram came out of the city; Laman, Lemuel, and Sam were scared and started to run away. Nephi called out to them. Zoram tried to run when he realized Nephi was not Laban. Nephi promised Zoram he would be safe if he went with them back to their father. They brought the brass plates back to their father Lehi.

Come Follow Me FHE
BOOK OF MORMON BASKET BOOK

Lehi's Dream

Lehi was a prophet. One day, he had a dream about his family. In his dream, he saw a tree with white fruit growing on it.

If someone ate the fruit on the tree, it made them happy. Lehi ate the fruit and it filled him with joy. He wanted his family to eat the fruit because he wanted them to feel the joy he felt.

Lehi saw his family at the end of the river that was flowing near the tree. He called to them to come taste the fruit. Lehi's wife, Sariah, and his sons Sam and Nephi went to Lehi and tasted the fruit and were happy.

Lehi's other two sons Laman and Lemuel would not taste the fruit. Lehi was worried for them.

In his dream, Lehi also saw a straight path and an iron rod leading to the tree.

Many people came to walk along the path. Some of them held firmly to the iron rod and were able to go to the tree and taste the fruit.

But because of a big mist of darkness, some people wandered off and were lost.

Lehi also saw a large building on the other side of the river. It was filled with people who were making fun of those who were eating the fruit.

Some of the people who ate the fruit did not like what the people in the building were saying about them. They were ashamed and left the tree to go to the building. They were not happy.

6

The people who stayed at the tree were happy. God's word is like the iron rod. When we follow His word, we will be happy.

Come Follow Me FHE
BOOK OF MORMON BASKET BOOK

Nephi Breaks His Bow

In the wilderness, Nephi and his brothers used bows and arrows to hunt for food.

1

One day while hunting, Nephi's steel bow broke, and his brother's bows lost their spring.

Nephi and his brothers could not kill any animals for their families, everyone was hungry. Laman and Lemuel were angry with Nephi for breaking his bow.

Nephi made a bow out of wood. Then he went to his father and asked him where he should go hunt.

Lehi prayed to Heavenly Father and asked where Nephi should go hunting. Lehi got directions from the Liahona.

Nephi followed the directions and found some animals for his family. When Nephi returned with the food everyone was happy. They were sorry they had been angry and they thanked God for blessing them.

Lehi and his family learned that the Liahona only worked when they were faithful, diligent, and obedient. (1 Nephi 16:28-29)

Come Follow Me FHE
BOOK OF MORMON BASKET BOOK

Nephi Builds a Ship

The Lord spoke to Nephi and asked him to build a ship to carry his family to the Promised Land. Nephi was nervous because he didn't know how to build a ship.

The Lord said He would help Nephi. He would show Nephi where to find the materials he would need to make tools to build the ship.

Nephi's brothers Laman and Lemuel made fun of Nephi for building a ship and they would not help him.

Nephi told Laman and Lemuel that the Lord would help him. He reminded them that they had seen an angel and that they should repent and remember that God has power to do all things. This made Laman and Lemuel angry.

Laman and Lemuel tried to grab Nephi to throw him into the sea. Nephi was filled with the power of God and commanded them not to touch him.

The Lord told Nephi to touch Laman and Lemuel. When he touched them, the Lord shocked them. After that, they knew that the Lord was with Nephi and that He was helping him. They repented and helped Nephi build the ship.

Nephi went to the mountain to pray many times and Heavenly Father helped Nephi to finish building the ship.

Come Follow Me FHE
BOOK OF MORMON BASKET BOOK

Enos

Enos was Jacob's son. One day he went into the forest to hunt.

While hunting Enos was thinking about what his father had taught about eternal life and the joy of the Saints. (Enos 1:1)

Enos wanted to have that joy. He knelt down and prayed to Heavenly Father. Enos prayed all day and into the night (Enos 1:4)

While he was praying, Enos heard the voice of the Heavenly Father say, "Enos, thy sins are forgiven thee, and thou shalt be blessed." (Enos 1:5)

Enos also prayed for the Nephites, Heavenly Father said they would also be blessed if they were righteous.

Then Enos prayed for his enemies, the Lamanites.

He also asked that the Nephite record would be kept safe and help the Lamanites one day.

Heavenly Father said He would do as Enos asked because of Enos's faith.

Come Follow Me FHE
BOOK OF MORMON BASKET BOOK

King Benjamin

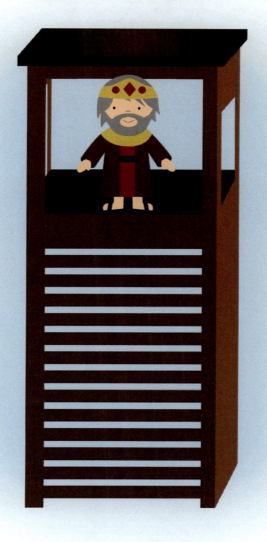

King Benjamin was a righteous leader. He wanted the Nephites to be happy.

He wanted to talk to his people to tell them that his son Mosiah would be the next king.

The people came from all over the land and pitched their tents near the temple.

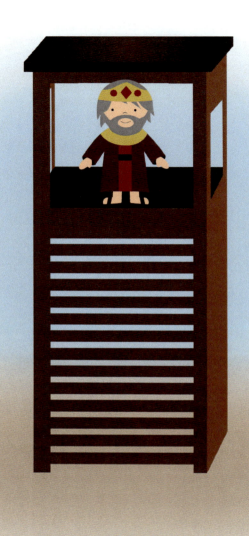

King Benjamin stood on a tower to speak so everyone could see and hear him.

He told the people that he loved them and that they should love and serve each other.

He taught them about the life of Jesus Christ and told them that if they followed Heavenly Father and kept His commandments they would be happy.

After he finished speaking, the Nephites fell to the ground to pray and repent for not always being obedient. Heavenly Father forgave them. They promised to keep the commandments.

King Benjamin told the people to teach their children to be obedient and to love and serve each other, and taught them many other good things.

He gave his son Mosiah the right to be the new king, and King Benjamin died three years later.

Mosiah was a righteous leader and loved and served his people just as his father had.

Come Follow Me FHE
BOOK OF MORMON BASKET BOOK

Abinadi

Abinadi was a prophet that the Lord sent to tell the wicked King Noah and his people to repent.

The people did not like what Abinadi was telling them and were angry. They brought Abinadi before King Noah and his priests.

The kings priest's questioned Abinadi. Abinadi answered all their questions and spoke boldly against their wickedness.

This made King Noah very angry, he ordered that Abinadi be put to death. (Mosiah 13:1) But Abinadi said, "God shall smite you if ye lay your hands upon me, for I have not delivered the message which the Lord sent me to deliver. (Mosiah 13:3)

Abinadi had the Lord's Spirit upon him and he spoke with power and authority. He taught the Ten Commandments, testified of Jesus Christ, and again called the people to repentance.

When Abinadi was done speaking King Noah was afraid of what he had said. King Noah had Abinadi put to death by fire. Abinadi gave his life as a witness of the truth (Mosiah 17:13-20)

Alma, one of King Noah's priests believed what Abinadi had said. He recorded Abinadi's words and taught the people in secret.

Come Follow Me FHE
BOOK OF MORMON BASKET BOOK

Alma the Younger

Alma the Younger did not believe what his father taught.

Alma the Younger and the four sons of King Mosiah told people that the church wasn't true.

Alma prayed for his son to learn the truth and repent.

One day, an angel appeared to Alma the Younger and the sons of Mosiah and told them to repent.

Alma was so shocked that he could not speak or move. He slept for two days and two nights.

When he woke up, he told the people that he had repented, and that God had forgiven him.

Alma the Younger and the sons of Mosiah began to teach the truth throughout the land, telling everyone about what happened to them.

Come Follow Me FHE
BOOK OF MORMON BASKET BOOK

Ammon Defends King Lamoni's Flocks

Ammon and his brothers served missions to the Lamanites.

Ammon offered to be King Lamoni's servant.
King Lamoni sent him to guard his flocks.

2

Wicked men came and scattered the king's flocks. The other servants were afraid they would be put to death because the flocks were lost.

Ammon convinced them to help him find the flocks.

When the wicked men came again to scatter the flocks Ammon told the other servants to keep the flocks together. Ammon fought the wicked men, he cut off the arms of the men that tried to attack him. Ammon was protected by the Lord.

The wicked men were afraid and ran away. King Lamoni heard what Ammon had done to protect his flocks. King Lamoni was amazed at Ammon's power.

Ammon told the king his power came from God. He taught King Lamoni the gospel, and the king believed.

Come Follow Me FHE
BOOK OF MORMON BASKET BOOK

The People of Ammon

The sons of Mosiah taught the gospel to the Lamanites. Many of the Lamanites repented and joined the church.

They called themselves Anti-Nephi-Lehies, or the people of Ammon.

The Lamanites who did not repent were angry with the people of Ammon. They wanted to fight them.

The people of Ammon had repented of killing. They did not want to fight back against the Lamanites.

They made a promise with God that they would never kill again and buried their weapons in the ground.

When the Lamanites came to fight, the people of Ammon did not fight back. They dropped to their knees and prayed that God would protect them.

The Lamanites saw that the people of Ammon were not fighting back, so they stopped fighting as well. They put down their weapons and joined the people of Ammon in their promise not to fight and kill anymore.

Come Follow Me FHE
BOOK OF MORMON BASKET BOOK

Captain Moroni

Amalickiah was a wicked man. He wanted to be king. He convinced many Nephites to support him.

Moroni was the Chief Commander of the Nephite army. He was angry when he heard Amalickiah was trying to convince the people to make him king. Moroni knew the people were in danger of losing their freedom.

Moroni tore his coat and wrote a message of freedom on it and raised it as a flag. He called it the title of liberty.

Moroni prayed for freedom in the land. He went among the people waving the title of liberty and calling on the Nephites to join him in protecting their freedom.

Amalickiah and his followers fled to join the Lamanites.

Others tried to run away also. Moroni stopped them and captured them. Most of those that Moroni captured promised to defend freedom.

Moroni placed a title of liberty on every tower in the Nephite land, and the Nephites again had peace. (Alma 46:35-37)

The people of Ammon had made a promise with God that they would not fight and kill anymore.

But, when their enemies attacked the Nephites, they wanted to break their promise and help the Nephites fight back.

Helaman did not want the people of Ammon to break their promise to God.

The sons of the people of Ammon had not made the same promise their fathers had made. They wanted to help the Nephites fight.

Helaman led two thousand brave young men into battle and called them his sons.

The sons of Helaman had never fought before, but they were not afraid. They said that their mothers had taught them to have faith in God.

The sons of Helaman fought bravely. After the battle was over, Helaman found that all two thousand of them had survived. Helaman knew that God had protected them.

Come Follow Me FHE
BOOK OF MORMON BASKET BOOK

Samuel the Lamanite

Samuel was a Lamanite prophet.
1

He preached repentance to the Nephites in Zarahemla. They did not like that he was telling them to repent so they kicked him out of the city.

The Lord told Samuel to return to the land of Zarahemla and tell the people to repent.

The people would not let Samuel back into the city.

4

Samuel climbed up on top of the city wall. He preached repentance and also prophesied about the signs that would accompany Jesus Christ's birth and death and told the people about His Resurrection.

Some of the Nephites believed what Samuel was preaching, but others were angry and threw stones and shot arrows at Samuel. The Lord protected Samuel from the stones and arrows.

The Nephites tried to capture Samuel, he was protected and jumped from the wall and fled back to his land.

Come Follow Me FHE
BOOK OF MORMON BASKET BOOK

Signs of Christ's Death

Some people watched for the signs of Christ's death. Some people did not believe the signs would come.

One day, there was a fierce storm. Thunder boomed and lightning flashed.

There were cities catching on fire, sinking into the sea, and being buried into the earth.

An earthquake began shaking the earth. Cities were destroyed, and many people were killed.

When the storm and earthquake stopped, a thick darkness covered the earth for three days.

The people were upset because of all of the destruction. They wished that they had repented of their sins.

Then they heard the voice of Jesus Christ. He told them that the most wicked people had been killed, and that those who survived should repent of their sins.

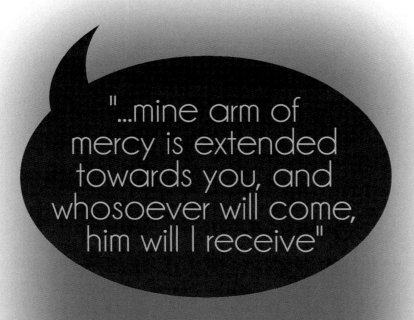

He told them that if they repented now, they could return to live with him. The people repented and thanked the Lord.

Come Follow Me FHE
BOOK OF MORMON BASKET BOOK

Jesus Christ Visits the Nephites

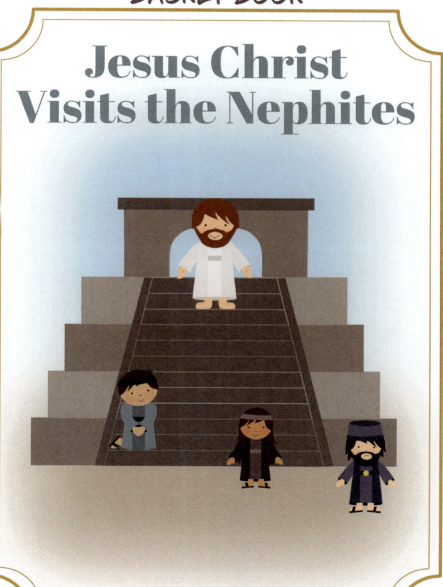

Many of the Nephites gathered at the temple after they experienced the three days of darkness. The people were talking about Jesus Christ and signs of his death.

1

While they were gathered they heard a quiet voice that made their hearts burn, but they didn't understand the voice. They heard the voice three times before they understood what it was saying.

The voice they heard was Heavenly Father introducing Jesus Christ. Heavenly Father told the people to listen to Jesus.

Jesus Christ came down from heaven and stood among the Nephites. He told them to come feel the prints in his hands, feet, and side.

Jesus taught the people many things. He also called 12 men to be disciples, so they could teach and baptize the people.

Jesus told them to bring those who were sick or hurt so he could heal them.

Jesus also told them to bring their children so he could bless them. Jesus loved the Nephites and told them to believe in Him, repent, and keep the commandments so they could enter His kingdom.

Come Follow Me FHE
BOOK OF MORMON BASKET BOOK

The Three Nephites

Jesus asked his disciples what they wanted from him. Nine of his disciples said they wanted to be able to live with Christ after they die.

The other three disciples wanted to stay on the earth to teach the gospel forever. Jesus blessed them with the knowledge they would need, and their bodies were changed so they would not die.

They began preaching the gospel, but there were wicked people who did not like that.

The wicked people sent the three disciples to prison.

And they threw the three disciples into deep pits, but the power of God was with them and they were able to escape.

The power of God also protected them when they were thrown into fiery furnaces and into the dens of wild animals.

The three disciples continued to preach the gospel to the Nephites, and they are still preaching the gospel of Jesus Christ today.

Come Follow Me FHE
BOOK OF MORMON BASKET BOOK

Mormon

A righteous man named Ammaron had the sacred records. Heavenly Father told him to hide the sacred records so they would be safe.

1

Ammaron told Mormon, a young 10 year old boy, where the records were hidden. Ammaron knew he could trust Mormon. When Mormon was 24 he got the plates of Nephi and wrote about his people on them.

Mormon gathered his people to the land of Cumorah for one last battle with the Lamanites. Because the Lord commanded Mormon to protect the plates he buried some of them in the Hill Cumorah and he gave his son Moroni a few of the plates.

The battle was fierce, Mormon was so sad and cried out "O ye fair ones, how could ye have departed from the ways of the Lord! How could ye have rejected that Jesus, who stood with open arms to receive you! Behold, if ye had not done this, ye would not have fallen." (Mormon 6:17-18)

Mormon wrote to the Lamanites about the latter days, telling them to repent and believe in Jesus Christ. To be baptized and receive the Holy Ghost. He said if they would do these things, they would be blessed in the Day of Judgment.

The Lamanites hunted and killed the remaining Nephites, including Mormon. Only Moroni was left.

After Mormon died, Moroni was alone. He finished the records his father had given him. He wrote that if people love God and follow him, they can become perfect. Moroni knew that one day the gold plates would be taken out of the ground and translated.

Come Follow Me FHE
BOOK OF MORMON BASKET BOOK

The Brother of Jared

Jared and his brother lived in a city called Babel. Most of the people in Babel were wicked.

The Lord told the brother of Jared to gather his family and leave Babel. He would lead them to a promised land.

The Jaredites took their animals and all kinds of seeds, birds, and fish with them.

While the Jaredites camped by the sea, the Lord told the brother of Jared to build some ships to take them across the ocean to the promised land.

The ships needed to be made so that no water could get in, but the brother of Jared didn't know how the people inside the ships would be able to get air or light.

The Lord told him to make two holes in each ship that could be opened and closed to let air in and keep water out.

4

The brother of Jared took 16 small stones to the top of a mountain and prayed. He asked the Lord to touch the stones so they would give light inside the ships.

The Lord reached out and touched each stone with his finger. Because of the brother of Jared's faith, he was able to see the hand of the Lord.

Now the brother of Jared was able to take the Jaredites safely across the ocean.

Made in the USA
Las Vegas, NV
28 December 2023